1346

920
WIL

Williams, Brian
Pioneers of flight

$18.60

DATE			
NOV 30 1995			

BAKER & TAYLOR BOOKS

□ PIONEERS OF FLIGHT □

Coxwell and Glaisher hang on for dear life during their record balloon flight of 1862.

TALES OF COURAGE

□

PIONEERS OF FLIGHT

□

BY BRIAN WILLIAMS

Illustrated by Francis Phillipps

□

STECK-VAUGHN
L I B R A R Y
A Division of Steck-Vaughn Company

Austin, Texas

Published in the United States in 1990
by Steck-Vaughn Co., Austin, Texas,
a subsidiary of National Education Corporation.

A Cherrytree Book

Designed and produced by
A S Publishing

Copyright © Cherrytree Press Ltd 1989

Picture Credits: pps 7, 8, 9 Mary Evans
Picture Library; pps 15, 24, 43 (top)
Jean-Loup Charmet; p26 The Illustrated
London News Picture Library; p27
bildarchiv preussischer kulturbesitz; p37
OM; p43 Frank Spooner Pictures; pps 44,
45, 46 Military Archive and Research
Services.

Library of Congress Cataloging-in-Publication Data

Williams, Brian.
    Pioneers of flight / by Brian Williams: illustrated by Francis Phillipps.
        p.   cm. — (Tales of courage)
    Summary: Presents a history of flight by narrating the
accomplishments of courageous men and women in the field.
    ISBN 0-8114-2755-2
    1. Aeronautics—History—Juvenile literature. 2. Astronautics–
–History—Juvenile literature. [1. Air pilots. 2. Aeronautics–
–Biography. 3. Astronautics—Biography. 4. Aeronautics—History.
5. Astronautics—History.] I. Phillipps, Francis, ill. II. Title. III. Series.
TL147.W535 1990
629.13′092′2—dc20
[B]   90-9470
[920]   CIP
                                                                                AC

Printed in Italy by New Interlitho
Bound in the United States by Lake Book, Melrose Park, IL
1 2 3 4 5 6 7 8 9 0 IL 94 93 92 91 90

□ CONTENTS □

□ PIONEERS OF FLIGHT □

Today, when air travel is commonplace, it is hard to recall that until this century no airplane had ever flown. For thousands of years people had dreamed of flying like birds. A few, perhaps as crazy as they were brave, strapped on birdlike wings and, like Icarus of the Greek legend, tried to fly. They leaped from towers and cliffs, and fell to their deaths.

According to the legend, Icarus was the son of the inventor Daedalus, who devised wings made from feathers and wax. Together they flew over the Aegean Sea, but Icarus flew too near the sun; its heat melted the wax in his wings and he fell into the sea and was drowned. The example of Icarus was often cited by those who believed that human beings were earthbound by divine intention; to attempt to conquer the air was to court disaster.

Into the unknown

The science of flight did not begin to be understood until 200 years ago. The Chinese flew kites and fired gunpowder rockets, but their ambitions went no further. Leonardo da Vinci drew a sketch of a flapping-wing airplane and a helicopter in the 1500s, but no engine had been invented that had the power to lift such aircraft into the air. Not until 1783 when the Montgolfier brothers recognized the lifting properties of hot air, and made a balloon, were human beings at last able to venture into the skies.

It is difficult for a modern person, used to high-speed travel by road and rail, as well as by plane, to understand how brave the first aeronauts must have been. In 1783 the steam railroad locomotive and the motor car had not been invented. No one had traveled faster than a horse could gallop. No doctor knew what effect flying might have on the body. The first balloonists soared aloft to explore a strange and unpredictable environment. Many lost their lives.

In 1853 Sir George Cayley, an English scientist, built a curious-looking winged machine. It was based on a model glider he had played with almost 50 years earlier. Sir George wanted to see if this large version would fly with a human passenger. His coachman was told to "volunteer" for the honor, and the poor man (no doubt quaking in his boots) duly did so. His bravery was no less than that of those who later earned the admiration of the world for their flying exploits.

Defying the doubters

The pioneers of the 1800s were often mocked. Their machines were fanciful and often collapsed spectacularly without ever leaving the ground. Only balloons, and the airships (steerable balloons with engines) that were developed from the 1850s on, seemed able to master the air. Thanks to the lonely, dangerous researches of men like Otto Lilienthal, knowledge of winged flight advanced, enabling the Wright brothers to make their short, but historic, flight in 1903. Those who followed the Wrights into the air flew in machines that were primitive by today's standards.

In 1910 George Chavez of Peru be-

Early balloonists often crash-landed with alarming consequences. This 1906 German aeronaut had a close call with a train.

came the first to fly over the European Alps. He flew through the Simplon Pass which is some 6,500 feet above sea level (his plane could not climb high enough to fly over the mountains). Tossed violently by swirling air currents, he was in sight of Italy when his machine buckled under the stresses to which it had been subjected. The little Blériot airplane simply collapsed, with wings folded, and Chavez tumbled to his death.

In 1919 Ernest Hoy flew over the Canadian Rocky Mountains in a 1914 vintage training aircraft. Its range was laughably short, but somehow Hoy made it, scraping through the Crawford Pass with only a few feet of air between

his aircraft and the jagged peaks below. In 1933 the Lady Houston Everest flight took the first aerial photographs of Mt. Everest, the world's highest mountain. The two Westland aircraft cleared the peak by just 100 feet.

Flying into danger

Such feats excited public interest in flying. But the general public knew little of the dangers involved. Aircraft engines were underpowered and unreliable. Bad weather, especially storms and headwinds, could be fatal, since no aircraft could fly high enough to avoid it. Many flyers crashed when overcome by exhaustion after many hours at the con-

Left: Two British Westland airplanes took the first air photos of Mt. Everest in 1933.

Right: French pilots Charles Nungasser and François Coli disappeared while trying to fly the Atlantic in 1927, in an aircraft like this.

trols. On long ocean crossings aircraft sometimes vanished without trace, with no radio or radar to track them. They flew into mountains, crashed on take-off when overweight with extra fuel, or became lost in fog or storms.

Without navigational aids, pilots often relied on ground landmarks — following railroad tracks or roads, or signs painted on barn roofs. Francis Chichester, flying across the Tasman Sea between Australia and New Zealand in 1931, used a sextant to take sightings of the sun. Experts had said no pilot could handle a sextant and fly at the same time. Even when he reached his stopover point, the tiny Lord Howe Island, Chichester faced the kind of problem that many air pioneers suffered. His DH

Gipsy Moth seaplane sank in a gale and had to be raised and repaired with the assistance of the islanders. Neither they, nor he, knew much — if anything — about how an airplane was constructed.

Charles Lindbergh, the first pilot to fly the Atlantic solo, in 1927, was one of many willing to risk such a dangerous journey. On May 8, 1927, two French pilots, Charles Nungasser and François Coli, took off from Paris intent on flying from France to the United States. Their biplane had enough fuel for 43 hours, but the wind over the Atlantic was against them, cutting their speed to only 75 miles per hour. At that slow speed, they would have run out of fuel more than 370 miles from the safety of the American coast. Their fate remains unknown.

Their courage, our comfort

There were many examples of amazing courage by men and women aviators during the pioneer years before World War II. In 1931 Ruth Nichols set a new women's altitude record of 28,743 feet. Her primitive breathing apparatus consisted of an oxygen tank and a rubber hose. The oxygen was so cold that it froze the inside of her mouth. A month later, she crashed her plane, badly injuring her back. Doctors told her not to fly for a year, but within two months she was back in the air, heavily plastered, for an Atlantic attempt.

Such was the determination that sent aviation pioneers flying around the world, opening up air routes to South America, Asia, and Australia. Their pioneer flights made possible the regular international airline services that we take for granted today. After World War II came the jet age, and a new generation of air pioneers: the test pilots. They flew aircraft faster and higher than ever before, into the fringes of space. They experienced the sonic boom and the effects of high stress forces on the human body. They tested ejector seats that were to save the lives of hundreds of jet pilots. Some joined the first corps of astronauts.

As you sit comfortably in your airline seat, watching a movie or enjoying the view across the clouds below, remember those who made it possible: the men and women who battled their way into the air. Their courage and perseverance made possible today's age of flying.

☐ THE FIRST AERONAUTS ☐

Could it be true? The watching crowds gasped in amazement as the yellow and blue balloon soared into the sky above Paris. Were men really flying? There was the proof: waving his hat triumphantly, Jean François Pilâtre de Rozier was fulfilling his vow to be the world's first aeronaut.

In 1782 a French papermaker named Joseph Montgolfier flew a model balloon indoors at his home at Avignon. The balloon was made of taffeta over a wooden frame and it was inflated with hot air from some twists of burning paper. From this humble beginning, Joseph and his brother Etienne progressed to bigger balloons that flew outdoors, and on June 4, 1783, they demonstrated their amazing new invention to their neighbors. It was a historic moment. After centuries of failure and disasters, people were about to take to the air. The human dream of imitating birds was, after all, to come true, thanks to the Montgolfiers' genius and the bravery of the first aeronauts.

By July the Montgolfiers were in Paris where they encountered a rival, the hydrogen-gas balloon being tested by Jacques Charles, the brilliant scientist. Charles flew his balloon first, on August 27, but the Montgolfiers went ahead with their preparations and on September 19 their balloon rose into the skies carrying with it the first aerial passengers — a sheep, a duck, and a rooster. King Louis XVI and Queen Marie Antoinette were among the amazed audience.

A young man eagerly sought out the Montgolfiers, pleading to be the first man to ascend in the wonderful balloon. Jean François Pilâtre de Rozier was ready to brave whatever unknown perils the flight might hold for a human. But King Louis had expressly forbidden any person to take part in flying experiments. His advisers warned that flying defied all natural laws: a man might explode in the thin air or go mad.

Pilâtre de Rozier was ready to defy even the royal veto. He was 26, a stout-hearted and scientific young man whose party trick was a fire-eating stunt, using hydrogen gas. A nobleman, the Marquis d'Arlandes, undertook to speak to the king on Pilâtre de Rozier's behalf — provided he too could fly in the Montgolfiers' balloon. Reluctantly, King Louis agreed and the Montgolfiers prepared their new balloon. It was 75 feet high and 50 feet in diameter, with a wickerwork gallery to carry the two aeronauts and an iron fire-basket to provide the hot air. Pilâtre de Rozier made several tethered test flights to heights of up to 325 feet in preparation for the great moment — the first free ascent.

The first ascent

The day chosen was November 21, 1783. A huge crowd gathered, many expecting to see the aeronauts suffer a dramatic death. Pilâtre de Rozier and d'Arlandes climbed into the basket beneath

The ropes were released and the huge crowd gasped as the balloon rose skyward.

the billowing balloon. They stood on opposite sides of the gallery, so as to balance the craft, facing away from each other. When all was ready, Pilâtre de Rozier gave the signal to the Montgolfiers on the ground. It was 1:54 p.m. The tethering ropes were released and at once the balloon rose into the air.

The aeronauts' hearts beat even faster, as the ground receded. Pilâtre de Rozier took a deep breath. The air was sweet, and he shouted with joy. The crowd, at first dumbstruck, burst into wild applause. The flyers doffed their hats and waved as the balloon soared into the sky.

Eager to climb higher, Pilâtre de Rozier urged his companion to throw more straw into the fire basket. Their only precaution against fire was a pail of water and a sponge — to dampen any scorch holes appearing in the balloon fabric. But danger was forgotten in the excitement of the moment. Below them lay Paris, as no one had ever seen it before, the streets jammed with people gazing upward at the astounding sight.

Back to earth — and up again
The flight lasted 25 minutes before the balloon drifted to earth, having traveled almost six miles. As it landed, the balloon collapsed around the aeronauts. A nobleman galloped excitedly to greet them; the three loaded the balloon onto a cart and drove back to Paris and a heroes' welcome.

Pilâtre de Rozier made several more flights, including one with Joseph Mont-

golfier (the inventor's only ascent) and five other passengers.

By 1785 balloonists had a new goal: to cross the English Channel. Pilâtre de Rozier visited London as the guest of the "British Balloon Club" and met another French flyer, Jean-Pierre Blanchard. He had announced plans for a Channel flight. Pilâtre de Rozier hurried back to France to prepare his own challenge.

Death of an aeronaut

For the Channel crossing, he decided on a combination of a Montgolfier hot air balloon below a hydrogen balloon. Since hydrogen is highly inflammable, the combination of an open fire and the gas was deadly. But Pilâtre de Rozier believed it would give extra height and endurance.

With a companion, Jules Romain, he took off from Boulogne early on a June morning in 1785. The balloon rose about 5,000 feet in the air. Then the horrified spectators (among them Pilâtre de Rozier's English fiancée, Susan Dyer) saw a puff of smoke, followed by a burst of flame. The hydrogen gas caught fire, and the Channel balloon plummeted earthward. Poor Pilâtre de Rozier was already dead when rescuers ran to the wreck. Romain died within minutes. So, too, did Susan Dyer, who collapsed from shock. It was a sad end to the life of the world's first fearless aeronaut.

The spectators could do nothing to save Pilâtre de Rozier and Romain, and fire rapidly consumed the wrecked balloon.

□ FLOATING HIGH □

Balloons were to dominate the story of flight in the nineteenth century. Balloon flying became fashionable. But danger was ever-present.

The first balloonists ventured into the sky with courage, but with little knowledge of how to control or navigate their craft. They were blown wherever the wind took them, and even if they did land unscathed they might face the wrath of an enraged, frightened mob. Several balloons were destroyed by villagers fearful of such an "ungodly machine."

The Montgolfiers' balloon carried with it the risk of fire, from the burning fire basket. The rival hydrogen balloon was even more dangerous, a flying bomb waiting to explode. But hydrogen was the only lighter-than-air gas available to the early flyers. Modern airships are filled with noninflammable helium gas.

Only days after Pilâtre de Rozier's historic first flight, Jacques Charles and Nicolas Robert ascended in their hydrogen-filled balloon. Half the population of Paris turned out to watch. Charles wrote afterward that "nothing will ever equal that moment of joyous excitement when I felt myself flying away from the earth." The balloon flew for two hours, before making a perfect landing 27 miles from its starting point. Charles was so thrilled he went up again, alone, even though it was after sunset. With only one passenger, the balloon shot up to a height (so Charles guessed) of 10,000 feet. He returned safely to earth, but he never flew again.

Across the English Channel

To be blown out across the sea was a balloonist's worst fear, for there was little hope of rescue.

Frenchman Jean-Pierre Blanchard was 31 when, in 1785, he set out to fly the English Channel. His companion (and sponsor) was John Jeffries, a Boston-born doctor. They took off from the Dover area on January 7 at 1:00 p.m. Much of their equipment soon had to be jettisoned, as the balloon dropped toward the sea. Over the side went aerial "oars," anchors, and the aeronauts' outer clothing. Blanchard even discarded his trousers, and both men put on cork life-jackets, fearing the worst.

Somehow, however, the balloon remained aloft and at 3:00 p.m. it crossed the coast of France. The two aerial pioneers landed in the treetops, some 12 miles inland.

Women take to the air

Some of the bravest pioneer balloonists were women. Elizabeth Thible of France was the first woman aloft, flying in a balloon in May 1784. A 14-year-old girl made the first ascent by a woman in England, as a passenger with Blanchard.

Blanchard's wife, Sophie, was an outstanding flyer. She was said to be happiest floating alone in a balloon, often ascending at night and sleeping in the air. Sophie Blanchard was another victim of the balloonists' greatest enemy: fire. She fell to her death when her balloon caught fire during an aerial fireworks display in 1817.

Higher and higher

In 1862 the scientist James Glaisher flew with Henry Coxwell, a British balloon pilot, to a height of over 32,000 feet (higher than Mount Everest). In the thin air and with no oxygen apparatus, they found breathing difficult, and could neither move nor speak. Even though he kept losing consciousness, Glaisher went on making scientific observations. Coxwell, his hands frozen, pulled at the release valve with his teeth to begin their descent to the ground. After landing, Glaisher walked 7.5 miles to the nearest town to hire a cart for the balloon!

Such bravery did much to increase scientists' knowledge of the upper air. But balloons would never provide reliable air transportation, dependent as they are on the winds. During the 1800s aviation pioneers wrestled with the seemingly insoluble problem of powered flight. Would it only be possible by fitting engines to a balloon – to make an airship? Or, was the answer to imitate the wings of birds and glide?

Blanchard was one of the first professional fliers, making exhibition flights all over Europe and the United States. This flight over Lille, France, took place shortly after his historic Channel crossing.

□ BIRDMAN □

Otto Lilienthal envied the birds. As a boy he watched them soaring in the skies and dreamed of imitating their flight. He became the most skillful "birdman" of the 1800s.

In 1848, when Otto Lilienthal was born in Germany, no one knew about winged flight. Balloonists shifted with the wind. Steam-driven planes puffed and roared, but failed to get airborne. Lilienthal dreamed of gliding, like the birds. He set out to discover how it could be done, building batlike gliders and testing them himself. Once airborne, he had to discover how to control his glider — or crash. His was a lonely, and very courageous, pioneering path to the skies.

Between 1891 and 1896 Lilienthal built a number of hang gliders. He made thrilling leaps from hilltops, defying gravity as he swung like a circus trapeze artist below the glider. He built an artificial hill from which to launch himself into the air. His efforts were watched by wondering, puzzled onlookers. Most of them thought he was crazy.

Trusting to the air

Lilienthal knew that each flight was risky. He painstakingly checked each strut and wire of the glider before he took off. Strapped into the harness, the taut wings quivering in the breeze, he could feel the glider trying to lift. When he was ready, he launched himself downhill, running to gain take-off speed until with a jerk his feet left the ground. The glider was flying. As the wind sang in the wires, Lilienthal could gaze down and experience the rare silent thrill of glider flight. His dream had come true: he was flying like a bird.

People were amazed at Lilienthal's daring. But few bystanders could appreciate the dangers, or the extent of his skill. He had learned to "fly" the hard way, by trial and error, using his body to control the glider. All the time he knew that a sudden wind gust could be fatal.

Lilienthal might have gone on to build a glider with an engine: the world's first true airplane. But the death he had

cheated so long finally found him in August 1896. His monoplane glider flipped over in midair and crashed to earth. The great glider pioneer was killed. Others would have to finish his work.

Others will follow

Lilienthal's courage and persistence inspired a Scottish glider enthusiast, Percy Pilcher. He built his own hang glider, the *Hawk*. In 1896 Pilcher designed a plane with an engine, but it never flew, for in 1899 he, too, was killed gliding.

It was left to an American, Octave

Lilienthal seemed to defy gravity as he soared aloft. Each flight was risky, and his body bore bruises from numerous crash landings.

Chanute, to ensure that such courageous deeds were not in vain. Chanute, the author of the first real history of aviation titled *Progress in Flying Machines*, also built an improved hang glider, based on Lilienthal's designs. He became friendly with two young Americans who had notions of their own about how to build flying machines. They were the brothers Wilbur and Orville Wright.

□ THE FIRST FLYERS □

Two young Americans set out to master the science of powered flight. They had begun as bicycle engineers. But their vision and dogged determination took their flying machine into the air one day in December 1903.

Wilbur and Orville Wright ran a bicycle shop and repair business in Dayton, Ohio. One day, Wilbur read a magazine article describing the glider experiments of the German, Otto Lilienthal. He was sure he and his brother could do better. But Lilienthal was dead, killed while gliding. The history of aviation was littered with tales of brave inventors who had crashed to their deaths in flying machines that simply would not work. Why risk your neck when you could make a living building bicycles?

Today, aircraft are designed and built by huge corporations owning vast factories and laboratories. Thousands of people work on each new design. In the early 1900s the aviation industry did not exist and motor cars were built one by one, by hand. There was nothing to stop Wilbur and Orville from designing their own flying machine – except fear of the

unknown and the ridicule of their neighbors. Many people at the time thought building an airplane was crazy.

Flying their gliders

The Wrights displayed a cool, level-headed courage in tackling the challenge. They dedicated themselves to overcoming the problems, working long hours day and night. They pored over calculations and drawings, and built gliders to see if the theory worked in practice.

The Wrights took their gliders to the Kill Devil sandhills of Kitty Hawk in North Carolina. They traveled there each autumn with the glider in pieces, assembled it, and flew it. Then they went home, to work on improvements. Their third glider, flown in 1902, had done well. But could such a machine be fitted with an engine and still fly?

The Wrights are proved right

Other inventors, such as fellow American Samuel Pierpoint Langley, were known to be working on aircraft designs. The newspapers reported crashes and accidents involving "flying machines." Few people really believed these weird machines would actually work.

Wilbur and Orville kept working steadily. They built their own gasoline engine because no existing engine was light enough. They designed and made

The Wrights' gliders looked like huge box kites. The brothers gained valuable experience flying these flimsy aircraft.

the twin airscrews for their new machine. They even constructed a wind tunnel to test the wing shape. By late 1903 they were ready to try it out in the air.

The brothers took their machine, named *Flyer,* to the Kill Devil hills. It was a lonely spot, away from prying eyes. There were no cheering crowds or journalists. On December 14 Wilbur stretched out in the pilot's position on the flimsy wing. The engine fired, but the *Flyer* would not lift off the ground. But the Wrights did not give up easily. On December 17 they tried again.

This time Orville was to be the pilot. Both men were dressed smartly, in suits, starched collars, and caps. Together, they checked the *Flyer* for the last time and fiddled with the engine. Then they talked quietly for a moment and shook hands. It might be their last handshake.

It was a cold, windy, rainy day. At 10:30 in the morning, Wilbur raised a flag to give the signal. Flat on his stomach on the left (port) wing, Orville waved to show he was ready and released the wire holding the aircraft onto its launch rail. Wilbur ran alongside to hold the right wing steady, fearing a sudden gust of wind would send the craft careering sideways. Orville stared ahead through the humming wires with his heart beating faster. The *Flyer* seemed suddenly to have a life of its own.

The machine ran along the launch rail for about 50 feet at a little over a fast walking pace. And then it lifted into the air. Orville felt the motion change, as the machine left the ground and took to the

Orville and Wilbur took turns piloting the Flyer *on their first exhilarating flights. The longest flight that day in 1903 lasted just 59 seconds.*

20

air under its own power. Wilbur released the wing and the *Flyer* flew. It rose to a height of only 10 feet, dipped, then climbed again before diving to the ground some 120 feet away.

Wilbur dashed to greet his brother, who climbed from the aircraft, breathless but grinning. Only five other people (from the nearby lifeboat station) watched the Wrights make history.

Triumphant, the brothers were eager to try again. The *Flyer* flew three more times that day. On the last flight, Wilbur flew for over 850 feet. Then the brothers packed up, sent a telegram home, and returned to work. The world had entered a new age.

Showing the world

Flying in a balloon or floating airship was very different from flying in an airplane, which is heavier than air and needs to be balanced exactly if it is not to crash headlong. Lift, thrust, drag: these were all unknown forces, to be investigated and understood. No one knew how to fly an airplane safely. How did

On September 17, 1908, Orville was badly injured when his plane crashed. His passenger, Army Lieutenant William Selfridge, was killed.

you climb? Turn? Slow down? How high could you fly? How fast? Every landing was a new adventure, every take-off a renewed challenge to the pilot's courage and skill.

The Wrights were soon venturing higher and staying aloft longer. In 1908 Wilbur took their new biplane to Europe and astonished people with his daring, flying for as long as two and a half hours, and even carrying passengers.

Other aviators followed where the Wrights had led the way. Soon airplanes were taking to the air across the United States and Europe, their pilots inspired by the pioneers of Kitty Hawk. After 1912 Orville Wright worked alone, because Wilbur fell ill with typhoid fever and died. Orville sold the business in 1915, and left aviation to others. He died in 1948, having seen the dawning of a new age: that of jets and rockets.

◻ DARING TO BE FIRST ◻

The Wrights had proved that the airplane could fly. In the years following their success, a small band of brave men and women followed them into the skies. These pioneer pilots had the courage to go where few others dared.

The race across the Channel

To fly over the sea in a machine made of wood and fabric, driven by a small, unreliable gasoline engine, called for real determination. Yet only six years after the Wrights' first flight, aviators were pitting themselves against this challenge.

The English Channel is not very wide (the white cliffs of Dover can be seen from France on a clear day), but its bad weather is notorious. It was a formidable barrier for the early airplanes and a psychological challenge for their pilots. Many people still believed the airplane was a toy, a kind of overgrown kite with a propeller. The British *Daily Mail* newspaper offered a cash prize for the first pilot brave (or foolhardy) enough to fly the Channel.

Among the leading pilots in Europe was Hubert Latham (French but of English descent). He took off from France on July 19, 1909, in an Antoinette aircraft with a tiny 50-hp engine. About 11 miles from Sangatte, the engine quit and Latham glided down to crash-land in the sea. Fortunately, the weather was calm and he sat on his floating aircraft, smoking a cigarette, until a rescue boat reached him.

Down, but not drowned: Hubert Latham awaits rescue in the English Channel.

▫ LOUIS BLÉRIOT ▫

Blériot landed in a field near Dover Castle. Flag-waving early risers greeted his spectacular arrival.

Next to try was Louis Blériot (bankrupt and nursing a foot burned by a hot exhaust pipe during an earlier flight). His monoplane had an engine even smaller than Latham's and his only guide to a safe landing place in England was a picture postcard sent by a friendly reporter.

Blériot took off at 4:41 in the morning of July 25, 1909, crutches strapped to the side of the plane! "Now I thought only of my machine . . .", he recalled later. Were his tiny engine to fail, he knew he could not glide down, since the plane could fly no higher than a few feet above the water. He must have listened anxiously to the engine's beat as he sat in the open cockpit, head and shoulders exposed above the flimsy, fabric-covered fuselage, peering over the wing and past the whirling propeller for sight of land.

He followed three ships heading for Dover, to make sure he did not lose his way and fly out into the bleak North Sea. Ahead lay the formidable 325-foot-high Shakespeare Cliff at Dover; Blériot's plane could not fly above such an obstacle, so he had to sideslip through a gap in the cliff edge before touching down in a field. It was 5:18 a.m. He had flown from France to England (24 miles) in just 37 minutes.

▫ First Across the U.S. ▫

The years before World War I were the years when pilots attempted the impossible almost every time they took off. No pilot surmounted more mishaps, in the air and on the ground, than Calbraith Perry Rodgers – the first man to fly across the United States.

The year was 1911. Rodgers' plane was a Wright machine, named the *Vin Viz Flyer*. His plan was to fly from New York to California, in a series of "hops." He would have to find fields to land in (there were hardly any airstrips), and pick his way across a continent. He aimed to follow the railroad, to show that airplanes were the future as far as transcontinental travel was concerned.

Rodgers' resolution was sorely tested. On only the second leg of his flight, he crashed into a chicken coop, and his plane had to be rebuilt by the Wrights' mechanic, Charlie Taylor.

Rodgers battled on against a series of setbacks. A spark plug popped loose from the engine, and he had to fly one-handed while holding it in place. He became lost in a thunderstorm, flying through crackling lightning. He suffered some 70 crashes before, after 84 days, he reached his destination, limping from the battered aircraft on crutches. His airplane had been practically rebuilt en route; only the rudder was left intact. But Rodgers had made it.

▫ Women Aloft ▫

The first woman pilot was Raymonde de Laroche of France. She was taught to fly in 1909 by Charles Voisin, the great French aircraft designer, when she was only 23 years old. In those days there was no dual control system for teaching pilots. The student sat in the cockpit at the controls while the instructor called out instructions from the ground. Once in the air, and out of earshot, the learner was alone with the aircraft and the elements. Flying needed a lot of courage. It was dangerous, Raymonde de Laroche agreed, but she regarded it as simply packing all the hazards of a lifetime into a few hours or minutes.

Other women pilots followed her lead. In 1911 American journalist Harriet Quimby became the first licensed woman pilot in the United States. Her friend Mathilde Moisant became number two, even though her brother John had met his death in a flying accident.

The daring Harriet Quimby
Harriet Quimby believed in flying, both as a sport and as the transportation of the future. In 1912 she traveled to England to attempt a cross-Channel flight, determined to show everyone what women pilots could achieve.

Harriet Quimby in her flying clothes. She believed flying offered women new opportunities.

She had been flying for only a year. She had no experience of flying over the open sea, or of navigation. It must have been daunting, waiting to take off on a damp, cold April day. She shivered, in spite of the extra clothing she was wearing beneath her flying suit. Friends gave her a hot-water bottle to strap around her waist to ward off the cold. She was also shown how to use a compass. Then she was in the air – and on her own.

Bad weather for flying

Unlike Blériot, Harriet Quimby was unlucky with the Channel weather. She flew into a cold, dense fog. She could see neither sky ahead nor sea below: she had little chance of following the tugboat that was supposed to act as her guide. Getting lost would be disastrous. Her plane had little reserve fuel and if she was forced down into the sea she could not survive long in the freezing water. She climbed higher to find a break in the fog, but fuel flooded the carburetor and her engine misfired. Her heart sank; below her was the cold, gray Channel.

As the tiny plane spiraled downward, she peered through her goggles at the waves, white-capped and menacing. But then the engine revived and she came out of the fog into sunlight. The Blériot skimmed low over the waves and to Harriet's intense relief she spotted the French coast. She managed to land on the beach, some 25 miles off-course from her target, Calais, and was greeted by a cheering crowd of fishermen.

Tragically, in July of that same year Harriet Quimby was killed during an exhibition flight near Boston. Her plane went into a sudden dive and both she and her passenger were flung out and killed.

THE AIRSHIP AVIATORS

A German engineer, Count Ferdinand von Zeppelin, pioneered the airship. The German zeppelin crews of World War I faced hardship and danger high in the sky.

The most advanced zeppelins flew very high to avoid enemy fighter planes – up to 23,000 feet. They were huge (more than 650 feet long) but slow, cruising through the clouds at less than 95 mph, like vast aerial whales. The crews of the zeppelins endured constant biting wind and freezing cold. Inside the gondolas, suspended beneath the vast gas envelope, the men wore layers of thick clothing, with newspapers stuffed inside for extra warmth.

Because of the risk of explosion from the highly inflammable hydrogen gas in the airship's gas cells, cooking was forbidden. The men ate cold sausage and bread, supplemented by chemically self-heating cans of stew. At maximum height, the crews suffered from altitude sickness, becoming so weak they could move only with difficulty. Occasionally an airship commander might order a below-cloud observation, lowering a man in a small gondola at the end of a long cable – surely one of the most perilous and uncomfortable assignments!

The airship was developed in the 1800s by pioneers such as Henri Giffard and Alberto Santos-Dumont. It had the advantages of long range and endurance, but a basic weakness was the hydrogen to inflate it. A zeppelin explosion in Lakehurst, NJ, among others brought airship travel to an end in the 1930s.

Zeppelin crews suffered from altitude sickness and numbing cold. They faced the threat of enemy bombs from above and machine-gun fire from below.

☐ AIRPLANES CAN MAKE IT ☐

Few people believed the flimsy airplanes of the 1910-1920 era could fly an ocean or cross the polar wastes. Only the pilots, willing it to be possible, believed airplanes could make it. They opened the way for our comfortable airline services.

Flying over the Atlantic today, a passenger sits high above the clouds and weather in a pressurized metal cabin. In six or seven hours, or less by the Concorde, the Atlantic Ocean is crossed possibly without a glimpse of the ocean. It was very different for the crews of three American flying boats who set off in May 1919 from Long Island, New York.

A flying boat had one big advantage over a landplane; it could touch down on the water if it ran out of fuel – if the sea was calm enough. The U.S. Navy's

The U.S. Navy flying boats ride out the Atlantic storms.

Alcock and Brown take off from Newfoundland for their 16½-hour flight to Ireland.

NC-class flying boats did not have the range to fly the Atlantic nonstop. They had to fly in legs, stopping to refuel. Fifty-seven naval ships were positioned across the ocean to aid the flyers.

The Atlantic proved a violent opponent. Two of the flying boats were forced down by bad weather and mechanical problems. One was abandoned at sea; the other had to taxi, using engine power, through rolling seas for 48 hours before reaching the Azores. Only one aircraft, NC-4, commanded by Lieutenant-Commander Albert Read, made the crossing, touching down first in Portugal and then in England, on May 31.

□ ALCOCK AND BROWN □

Two weeks later, on June 14, 1919, two British flyers, John Alcock and Arthur Whitten Brown, set off from Newfoundland. Their aim was to fly the Altantic nonstop. There were to be no watery touchdowns for them, for their aircraft was a landplane, a Vickers Vimy bomber, with twin engines. The Vimy had a maximum range of 2,400 miles. Would this be enough? Ahead lay 1,860 miles of ocean, and then Ireland, their planned landing point.

The pilots' black cat mascot dolls, Twinkletoes and Lucky Jim, did not at first bring them much luck. They flew into fog, with thick clouds above. Their radio broke, and after an exhaust snapped on one engine the noise was so great neither man could hear the other shout.

The Vimy battles through

They flew very low (compared to modern planes) at between 3,250 and 6,500 feet and much slower – around 120 mph. Pilots had no instruments at this time for "blind" flying, so any large cloud posed real problems. For a while they had no idea where they were, until they climbed above the clouds into clear skies and could take a navigational sun sighting. It was bitterly cold. Brown had to stand up in the open cockpit to scrape snow off the fuel-flow indicators. Even the coffee in their flasks was little comfort.

At 8:30 a.m., June 15, they sighted Ireland, and because the weather was bad decided to land the moment they could. What looked like a green field turned out to be a soft bog, and the Vimy ended up with its tail in the air – an undignified end to an epic flight.

□ ATLANTIC ALONE □

Charles Lindbergh was the first person to make the long, dangerous Atlantic crossing alone. The danger of crashing at take-off, the risk of engine failure over the ocean, the likelihood that a lone pilot would fall victim to sheer weariness; all these were perils to be overcome.

It was May 20, 1927. Shortly after dawn, Charles Lindbergh had taken off from Roosevelt Field, New York. His destination: Europe. Before him lay the Atlantic Ocean and a flight into history.

As the small monoplane droned on through the empty skies above the Atlantic, Lindbergh had plenty of time to ponder over his chances of ever reaching land. Ahead lay vast stretches of cold, empty ocean. He had planned the flight with care, but so many things could go wrong. And there was no one to help if trouble struck.

A flying fuel tank

At least his plane, the *Spirit of St. Louis*, was his own choice for the flight. He had wanted a single-engined plane because it offered longer range. But if that one engine should fail, thousands of miles from land . . .

Lindbergh was confident it would not. Today, when aircraft are bigger, faster, and crammed with electronic navigation aids unknown in the 1920s, twin-engined jets must follow strict routes over long sea flights. Most trans-Atlantic airliners have three or four engines. Lindbergh had no such safety margin.

Sitting on his wicker seat in the cramped cockpit that measured just 37 inches wide by 32 inches long by 51 inches high, Lindbergh could not even see where he was going. His only forward vision was through a periscope. The *Spirit of St. Louis* was a flying fuel tank, with extra tanks added to give it the range to fly the Atlantic. The extra fuel was stored in front of the pilot, blocking his forward view. Lindbergh had asked for this: he felt safer with the fuel in front, fearful that a tank behind him might be forced forward and crush him in the event of a crash landing.

He knew that if it were to succeed, his flight would be a marathon of endurance. His only supplies consisted of two bottles of water and some sandwiches to sustain him over a distance of 3,600 miles—roughly twice the distance flown by Alcock and Brown in 1919.

The aircraft carried enough fuel for 40 hours' flying when it took off at 7:50 in the morning of May 20. Take-off was probably the most dangerous moment of such long-distance flights; weighed down by extra fuel, the aircraft rose uncertainly into the air, gaining height very slowly. Other flyers had met disaster at this point, so Lindbergh was relieved when the *Spirit of St. Louis* was safely aloft and cruising eastward.

Lindy's lonely odyssey

Lindbergh was attempting the dream of pioneer aviators. An Atlantic solo crossing would prove not only the reliability of the airplane, but also the dependabil-

Lindbergh sat hunched inside this tiny cockpit for 27 hours. He could see out of the aircraft only through a periscope or a side window.

ity of the human in the cockpit. But a lone pilot faced the ever-growing danger of exhaustion. Lindbergh, an experienced airmail flyer with the U.S. Post Office, knew the dangers of falling asleep at the controls. There was no automatic pilot to take over in those days.

As he left Newfoundland behind and headed out over the Atlantic, his mind began to wander. Would he forget to switch between fuel tanks, to keep the plane balanced? The engine seemed to be running rough, but he found it hard to concentrate on the rhythm. He was getting tired.

He slapped his face, forcing his eyelids upward with his fingertips, and leaned out of the cabin window so that the blast of freezing air shocked him back to wakefulness.

Having regained control of his weary senses, Lindbergh made himself work. He checked the wind, rechecked his course, and scanned the clouds through his periscope. The flight seemed endless; it was as if he had flown into a dreamworld, remote from reality. What am I doing here? he mused. Can I endure this? How much longer?

From the time Lindbergh left New

York, he had no means of contacting the world. His plane had no radio. There was no means of tracking it (radar was not yet invented). Unless a ship spotted him, he would be lost to view until he landed – if he landed. Bad weather was the worst enemy. If he was forced off course, he could become disoriented, lost in clouds, and circle vainly until his fuel ran out and the engine died.

Lindbergh's flight was a triumph of willpower. He flew through rain, storm winds, fog, and even snow. At times the *Spirit of St. Louis* flew only 100 feet above the water – Lindbergh became anxious that he might hit an iceberg and climbed to 10,000 feet until bad weather forced him down again. He could see porpoises in the sea beneath him. At one point he began seeing "mirages" of coastlines that were not there.

He could think only of sleep, and of stretching his aching limbs. He had been alone in the cockpit for 27 hours without seeing a sign of human life. At home people had gone to bed, gotten up, gone about their day's work, while he flew on, over the Atlantic.

Land ahoy!
The sight of fishing boats cheered him immensely. Europe must be close. He circled the boats, calling from the open cockpit: "Which way to Ireland?" There

was no answer, no crewman even appeared on deck. It was eerie.

At last, after 16 hours flying across unbroken ocean, he spotted land, real land. It was Ireland. He saw another fishing boat, and was given a friendly wave from a startled fisherman as the plane roared overhead. He had made it!

Turning southeast, he crossed the English Channel and flew over the coast of France. It was now the evening of May 21. Darkness was falling but Lindbergh's aircraft had been spotted, and people were streaming out of Paris to greet him. At 10:22 p.m. the *Spirit of St. Louis* dropped down from the night sky and landed on the airfield of Le Bourget.

The epic flight had taken 33 1/2 hours.

The plane rolled to a halt, and the engine died. The lights of cars and flashbulbs flared in the darkness. Charles Lindbergh, the flyer who had braved the wide ocean alone, climbed out of the cockpit and into the limelight. He was now the most famous man in the world.

One tragic consequence of Lindbergh's fame was the kidnapping of his infant son in 1932. The abducted child was found dead.

Lindbergh was cheered by excited crowds as he walked stiffly from the plane and into the glare of publicity that was to last for the rest of his life.

▫ WINGS ACROSS THE OCEAN ▫

By the 1930s some of the basic problems of flight had been tackled. The pioneers of aviation had advanced a little, but there was still a long way to go.

Courageous pilots, some with surprisingly little experience, set out to cross oceans and deserts, flying over mountains and forests, even over the Arctic and the high Himalayas. The dangers they faced were many: fatigue, engine failure, running out of fuel, simply getting lost without radio or radar to guide them, and with very few airstrips to head for in an emergency.

▫ THE AIRPLANE GIRL ▫

Amy Johnson was Britain's "air queen" of the 1930s. She learned to fly in 1929, and only a year later embarked on a flight that would have deterred a seasoned pilot. She planned to fly from Britain to Australia! Amy Johnson believed in aviation. She was willing to give up her job, and risk her life, to demonstrate that a lone pilot could open up an air route that thousands of passengers would one day be able to fly in comfort.

Her plane was a tiny, green-painted Gipsy Moth, named *Jason*. Her planned route was to take her across two continents and some of the wildest country on earth. There would be few airstrips to land on, and little chance of rescue should she come down in desolate mountains or tropical jungle. On the map it looked forbidding enough; the

Destination Australia: Amy Johnson prepares for departure from Croydon Aerodrome, England.

course was from England across Europe and the Middle East, across India to Bangkok and Singapore, and finally south over the islands of the East Indies and the open sea to Australia. She left England on May 5, 1930, cheered by a small crowd of friends and wellwishers.

Today, it is hard to imagine the problems Amy Johnson faced. She had to hand-pump almost 53 gallons of fuel each day. She was a skilled mechanic (mostly self-taught) but had to force male engineers to let her near the engine during refueling stops! Her plane could fly no higher than 10,000 feet, yet many of the mountains on her route were above this height. She had to find a path between the peaks.

Sand, sun, and sharks

Each leg of her journey brought new dangers. While flying across the Syrian desert her plane flew into a sandstorm. Whirling clouds of sand billowed upward, blinding her, forcing her to make an emergency landing before sand grains choked the engine. In Burma a damaged wing had to be patched with shirt material borrowed from a local tailor. By the time she reached Singapore, her face was burned brick-red by the sun and she was exhausted. Worst of all, the most difficult stage of the flight – over Indonesia and the Java Sea – still lay ahead. At one landing strip in the dense jungle, fuel cans were carried to the plane by donkey and she had to filter the gasoline herself to make sure it was safe to use. On the last leg, she had to cross the open ocean to reach northern Australia; she flew 500 nerve-racking miles over seas notorious for sharks. Finally she landed at Darwin on May 24, 1930.

Amy Johnson made other daring long-distance flights, including some with her husband Jim Mollison. She remained a celebrity of the air until her death in a wartime flying accident in 1941.

□ BERYL MARKHAM □

Imagine diving seaward, with no engine, trying desperately to turn on the reserve fuel tank of your plane! This was the situation the Kenya-born British flyer Beryl Markham faced in 1936. And she was alone above the Atlantic.

In the 1930s a small aircraft flying the Atlantic could easily be blown off course by strong head winds. Blowing directly against the aircraft's course, these winds could also slow down the airspeed so much that the aircraft ran out of fuel long before land was in sight. When Beryl Markham took off from Abingdon, England, in 1936 her Vega Gull aircraft had enough fuel for 24 hours at a speed of 150 mph – provided there was no head wind. She was trying to be the first woman to fly the Atlantic solo from east to west. Only Jim Mollison had done so, and he had started farther west, from Ireland.

Soon after take-off, Beryl Markham found herself flying into a 40-mph head wind. She battled on, grimly holding her course into the wind, yet aware that she was using more fuel than planned. Four hours after taking off, the engine stopped. In darkness, she groped for a flashlight to help her find the tap of the reserve fuel tank. The plane was only 230 feet above the waves when she found the tap, and the engine roared back to life.

more than 16,500 miles – in 8 days, 15 hours, and 51 minutes.

In their single-engined Lockheed Vega monoplane, Post and Gatty took off from Roosevelt Field, New York. They headed east stopping in Britain and Germany before the long flight across Russia, the wastelands of Siberia, and Alaska's frozen oceans. In Canada they were forced to take off from a road because an airfield was flooded.

By their remarkable feat of endurance and engine reliability, Post and Gatty proved that airplanes had the potential to fly regular passenger routes.

1930s aerial elegance: Beryl Markham symbolized the glamour of flying.

Markham had been in the air for more than 19 hours before she at last sighted the coast of Newfoundland. It was none too soon, for the engine was spluttering ominously. With a virtually empty fuel tank, the plane limped over the shoreland and crash-landed nose-first in a swamp. Beryl Markham managed to climb out of the cockpit. She was exhausted and waist-deep in mud when rescued by fishermen.

▫ GATTY AND POST ▫

In June 1931 American pilot Wiley Post, with Australian navigator Harold Gatty, flew around the world – a distance of

▫ ON A WING AND A PRAYER ▫

One of the most famous record-breaking pilots was Charles Kingsford Smith of Australia. In May 1935 he and navigator Gordon Taylor took off in the *Southern Cross* for an airmail flight to New Zealand, crossing the Tasman Sea.

It should have been a routine trip, but after 560 miles one of the aircraft's two engines failed, forcing them to turn back. Then the overworked port engine began to overheat, burning oil and losing power. The two men dumped cargo and excess fuel to save weight, but the plane gradually lost height until it was almost touching the waves.

Somehow they had to get oil into the engine. While Kingsford Smith flew as steadily as he could, Taylor crawled out of the cockpit with a vacuum flask of oil. He inched his way out along the wing, grimly holding on to the flask.

He did the same thing five times, every 35 minutes, filling up the sick engine with oil before the *Southern Cross* landed safely after 16 hours in the air.

AMERICA'S FLYING HEROINE

It was 1932. Alone in a small aircraft, the gray ocean surging beneath her, Amelia Earhart braved the angry elements. Many pilots believed that no woman could fly solo over long distances. Earhart was determined to prove them wrong.

Climb! Climb! As the storm buffeted her plane above the cold Atlantic Ocean, Amelia Earhart remembered the words of her flying instructor. Climb! Get above the bad weather – if you can. Since gaining her pilot's license in 1922 (when there were fewer than 20 women pilots in the world) Amelia Earhart had tackled a number of aerial challenges. She was one of a small but determined and skillful band of women aviators, whose record-breaking feats were even more remarkable because of the incredible physical demands long-distance flights made on a solo pilot.

Earhart is remembered above all for one flight, the solo crossing of the North Atlantic she made in 1932. As she piloted her Lockheed Vega eastward she must have thought of those who had said, "It can't be done, not by a woman!"

First woman to fly the Atlantic

Amelia Earhart was a born daredevil. Her mother had been the first woman to climb Pikes Peak, a mountain in Colorado, and Amelia inherited her adventurous spirit. As a young girl she had been entranced by the adventure of flight.

Earhart had learned to fly and in 1928 she became the first woman to cross the Atlantic in an airplane, as a passenger on board a Fokker Trimotor. After 20 hours in the air, the seaplane landed off the coast of Wales, and the aviators were surprised to find that for some time no one took any notice of them!

Determined to show that women could be pilots as well as passengers on long-distance flights, Earhart decided to fly the Atlantic herself – alone. Her husband, publisher George Putnam, helped buy her "dream plane," a red-painted Lockheed Vega with a range of just over 3,000 miles. It was the right aircraft for the flight, but even so the prospect was daunting. If Atlantic seas were wild, Atlantic weather was often wilder, and so far only two flyers (both men, Charles Lindbergh and Bert Hinkler) had flown the Atlantic alone. For a lone pilot the risks of accident or falling asleep at the controls were real on such a long flight, so far from land.

Braving the storm's force

"Do you think I can make it?" Earhart asked her friend and technical adviser Bernt Balchen as she squeezed herself into the pilot's seat. He nodded. But everyone knew what risks she was taking. Amelia remained calm, grabbing a last nap as the mechanics made the final adjustments to the Vega's engine and checked the extra fuel tanks in the wings and cabin.

Alone above the cold, stormy Atlantic Ocean, Earhart knew she stood little chance if the Vega's engine were to fail.

Amelia Earhart traveled light. Her few in-flight comforts included an elephant's foot bracelet for luck, a silk scarf, a screwdriver for punching holes in tomato juice cans, a flask of soup, smelling salts (to keep awake), and a powder compact so she could "look nice when the reporters come."

On May 20, 1932, the Lockheed took off from Harbour Grace, Newfoundland. Amelia Earhart took soup and cans of tomato juice for her only food supply: "Extra food would have been extra weight." She also took smelling salts to revive her when sleepy. If she were to crash into the sea, her best hope was to signal to a passing ship with an emergency flare.

Cruising at 13,000 feet, Amelia could enjoy the sunset. The engine droned reassuringly as she set course eastward, knowing it would be many hours before she could relax her concentration.

Before long, problems began. Besides fighting off tiredness, she had to cope with the discomforts of the cramped cabin and with the sickening smell of hot oil from the engine. Only hours after take-off, the plane's altimeter had failed, so for most of the flight she had no idea how high she was flying. Flames burst from a broken welding in the engine exhaust. The fire alarmed her, but even worse was the nerve-shattering vibration throughout the cabin. To add to her difficulties, there was yet another danger: the Atlantic weather.

Stormy weather

The aircraft of the 1930s flew through the weather, not above it like today's jets. They were tossed and spun like leaves in the wind. As Earhart's Vega battled onward, it pitched wildly and she had difficulty keeping control. Rain lashed the windshield, so that she could barely see the aircraft's propeller. Struggling to stay on course, she climbed higher to seek clearer weather. But to her horror she saw ice beginning to form on the wings. Icing could be fatal. If ice overloaded the wings, the plane would become unstable and crash. She must lose height again. Diving seaward in a near-vertical spin, back into the storm, the Vega narrowly escaped disaster, leveling out only feet above the waves. Thankfully, she gained height again.

The storm finally relented and the Vega's engine never faltered despite the broken weld, the flames, and the smell. Weariness was now the main threat. Amelia resorted to the smelling salts whenever she felt sleep threatening. Her body ached, and the pilot's seat now felt hard and unyielding.

At last she glimpsed a smudge of green on the horizon – land. After 13 1/2 hours, the Lockheed came down safely in a farmer's field at Culmore in Ireland. Earhart had flown the Atlantic, and she had done so faster than either Lindbergh or Hinkler. For a few weeks after her triumphant arrival in London she had to attend celebrations in her honor.

Triumphs and disaster

After her epic flight, Earhart was the most celebrated woman pilot in the world. She was eager to accept new challenges. In 1935 she made the first solo flight from Hawaii to California in 18 hours. In 1937 she set off with copilot Fred Noonan to fly around the world in a specially equipped Lockheed Electra.

On such long flights, safety margins were narrow. Exact navigation was essential if landfalls were to be found in the vast Pacific Ocean. Bad weather, poor visibility, instrument failure, fuel miscalculation: any of these could be fatal. On a 2,500-mile leg across the Pacific, radio contact with the aircraft was lost after 15 1/4 hours. The Lockheed had vanished. No trace of it, or of Amelia Earhart and Fred Noonan, was ever found. The most likely answer to the mystery is that Amelia became lost in fog, missing the island where she was due to land, and crashed into the sea when the plane's fuel ran out.

The Lockheed Electra made 28 stops on Earhart's round-the-world trip, some, like this one, enforced. Engineers worked around the clock to do repairs.

☐ TESTING THEIR COURAGE ☐

The pioneers of aviation were their own test pilots. Few knew even the rudiments of aerodynamics. They "flew into the unknown by the seat of their pants." Modern pilots still explore the unknown, in lightweight craft such as *Voyager,* in high-speed research jets, and in spacecraft such as the Space Shuttle.

In the 1930s and 1940s test pilots began to explore new and dangerous areas of flight. The first jets were taking to the air, beginning with Germany's He 178 in 1939. There were new and revolutionary aircraft designs on the drawing board. Someone had to fly each one for the first time. Hanna Reitsch, Germany's ace woman pilot, flew the FW-61 helicopter inside an auditorium and also piloted the "pilotless" V1 flying bomb.

In the early 1940s wartime fighters such as the Spitfire and Mustang represented the top of the line for piston-engined planes. Diving from 40,000 feet at speeds around Mach 0.89 (600 mph), they were flying at the limits of propeller-engined performance. Wings "fluttered," propellers sometimes broke up, and controls became stiff.

As the new jets came into service, speeds increased dramatically. Could a pilot survive such speeds? Would high G-forces (gravity) cause blackouts and prevent humans from ever passing the speed of sound? How could a pilot escape from an aircraft in trouble at these unheard-of heights and speeds?

There were many challenges for the test pilots of the late 1940s and 1950s. Some experts had predicted that supersonic flight was impossible; it would wreck aircraft and shatter the human body.

Those fears were disproved by Chuck Yeager, pilot of the rocket-powered Bell X-1. Inside this research aircraft, Captain Yeager became the first pilot to fly faster than sound, in 1947. There was no physical barrier, but supersonic flight called for new designs of aircraft, some of them very unusual.

The calculated risk

Test pilots had to take risks, pushing themselves and their jets to new limits. They often saw friends killed. British pilot John Derry tested the experimental DH 108 Swallow (a tailless design) in 1948. One prototype had exploded, killing its pilot Geoffrey de Havilland. But Derry continued the test program, calmly recording every detail during each flight. He put the plane into its steepest-ever dive and, less than a minute away from hitting the ground, became the first Briton to break the "sound barrier before pulling out."

Derry was killed at the Farnborough Air Show in 1952 when his DH 110 jet broke up during a high-speed flyover. A total of 28 spectators were killed in the crash. In the shocked moments following Derry's death, a fellow pilot, Neville Duke, took off in a Hunter and flew supersonically across the airfield — a characteristic tribute from one test pilot to another.

The same spirit of courage that inspired the pioneer aviators and the test pilots impels the pioneers of spaceflight. After the tragic accident in 1986 that killed seven *Challenger* astronauts, America and the world wondered if the Shuttles would ever fly again. After two years' work, a redesigned Shuttle went back into space. While in Earth orbit, 1988–89, Soviet cosmonauts set a new endurance record of 366 days in their space station. And so the story continues.

Round-the-world flyers Dick Rutan and Jeana Yeager of the United States traveled in considerable discomfort squeezed inside their "flying fuel tank."

How much faster can we go? The Bell rocket plane blasted through the sound barrier in 1947 and took aviation into a new era.

Beyond the limits

When Dick Rutan and Jeana Yeager took off from Edwards Air Force Base, California, in December 1986, they were attempting to make the first nonstop round-the-world flight. Their plane was the odd-looking and ultra-lightweight *Voyager*. In it the two stayed aloft for 9 days, 3 minutes, and 44 seconds to complete the historic flight, squeezed inside a fuselage too small to stand up in. Like the first flyers, they too were at the mercy of wind and weather, testing their own physical and mental endurance.

□ HIGH FLYERS □

Ader, Clément French pioneer of flight. His *Eole* airplane is reported to have "hopped" 165 feet in 1890.

Alcock, John and **Brown, Arthur Whitten** British pilots who made the first nonstop flight across the Atlantic (1919).

Barnstormers Daredevil stunt flyers of the 1920s who thrilled crowds by low-level flying, aerobatics, and displays including wing-walking and stunts in which people transferred from one plane to another in midair.

Batten, Jean New Zealander who was the first woman to fly across the dangerous Tasman Sea, and in 1936 flew from England to New Zealand in 11 days.

Blanchard, Jean-Pierre French balloonist, first to fly the English Channel (1785). Made the first balloon ascent in the U.S. from Philadelphia on January 9, 1793 – his 45th flight.

Blanchard, Sophie French balloonist, wife of Jean-Pierre Blanchard. Made her first ascent in 1805. Killed in 1817 when her balloon caught fire.

Blériot, Louis French pilot who made the first flight across the English Channel in an airplane (1909).

Byrd, Richard U.S. explorer, first to fly over the North Pole, with Floyd Bennett, in 1926. Also first to fly over the South Pole (with three companions) in 1929.

Cayley, Sir George British glider pioneer of the early 1800s, who flew models and tested a human-carrying version in 1853.

Cobham, Sir Alan British aviator who in the 1920s flew around Africa, from Cape Town to London, from London to Rangoon, and from England to Australia and back. Also pioneered in-flight refueling.

Cochran, Jacqueline U.S. flyer, first woman to break the sound barrier (1953); set 1974 women's speed record of 1,429 mph.

Cody, Samuel U.S. pilot who made first airplane flight in Great Britain, October 16, 1908.

Coleman, Bessie First black woman pilot, who went from the U.S. to France in order to learn. Killed flying in an air show in 1926.

Costes, Didier French flyer, first to fly nonstop across South Atlantic, from Senegal to Brazil (2,000 miles in 19 hours, 50 minutes, 1927).

Coxwell, Henry British balloonist, made a high-altitude ascent in 1862, flying higher than Mt. Everest.

Curtiss, Glenn First U.S. pilot to fly more than 2/3 mile in public (1908); invented the seaplane (1911).

Davies, E. Trehawke First woman to fly the English Channel, as a passenger with Gustav Hamel (1912).

Defries, Colin First man to fly an airplane in Australia (1909).

de Laroche, Raymonde French baroness, first woman to hold a pilot's license (1910).

Dirigible Steerable airship; the first fully controllable dirigible was the *La France* of Renard and Krebs (1884).

Doolittle, James H. U.S. pilot who made the first

Amelia Earhart – most famous of all women pilots.

coast-to-coast flight across the U.S. in a single day (1922). The first nonstop crossing of the U.S. was by O.G. Kelly and J.A. Macready in 1923 (2,516 miles in 26 hours, 50 minutes).

Earhart, Amelia Most famous of all women flyers; first woman to fly the Atlantic solo.

Farman, Henry British/French designer of some of the best early airplanes.

Garnerin, André Jacques French inventor of the first practical parachute (1797). His niece Eliza became the world's first female professional parachute jumper.

Glaisher, James Scientist who made a record balloon ascent with Coxwell at the age of 53, and died the same year as the Wrights flew (1903).

Hargrave, Lawrence Australian inventor of the box kite (1893).

Henson, W.S. British inventor of the Aerial Steam Carriage, an unsuccessful airplane of 1842-43.

Hinkler, Bert Australian pilot. First to fly solo from England to Australia (1928), second pilot to cross the Atlantic solo. Killed 1933.

Johnson, Amy British pilot whose epic flights of the 1930s made her an international celebrity. Flew solo from Britain to Australia. Set a 1936 record for the flight of 3 days, 16 1/2 hours.

Kingsford Smith, Sir Charles Australian aviation pioneer, first to fly from U.S. to Australia (7,270 miles) in 1928.

Langley, Samuel Pierpoint U.S. designer of the *Aerodrome*, which fell into the Potomac River in 1903 as it was launched.

Law, Ruth U.S. flyer, first woman to loop the loop and a record-breaker of the 1916 era.

Lindbergh, Charles U.S. pilot, first to fly the Atlantic solo (1927).

Markham, Beryl Kenya-based flyer who flew the North Atlantic solo in September 1936, crossing in 21 1/2 hours from Abingdon, England, to Nova Scotia.

Maxim, Sir Hiram British designer of a flying machine that just failed to fly in 1894.

Mock, Jerrie American flyer, the first woman to fly solo around the world (1964).

Mollison, Jim British aviator of the 1930s, flew the Atlantic from east to west. Married to Amy Johnson for a time.

Money, Major John English balloonist who was

Charles Kingsford Smith vanished in 1935 flying his Lady Southern Cross *from India to Singapore.*

Ruth Nichols, one of America's foremost "petticoat pilots." Her fur coat was no luxury in a freezing cockpit.

blown out across the North Sea in 1785 and spent five hours clinging to the wreckage before being picked up by a revenue cutter.

Nichols, Ruth American flyer who became known as the "Flying Deb" and set many flying records between 1928 and 1931. The first woman to land in every one of the then 48 states of the United States.

Norton, Richard U.S. flyer who, with Calin Rossetti, made the first single-engined flight around the world over the poles in 1987.

Oliver The so-called "Flying Monk of Malmesbury," said to have leaped from the Abbey Tower wearing wings in 1020. Broke his leg.

Pangborn, Clyde U.S. flyer, with Hugh Herndon, flew nonstop across the Pacific, from Japan to the U.S. (4,535 miles) in 1931.

Peltier, Therese French, first woman to fly in an airplane (as a passenger) in 1908 when she went aloft with Leon Delagrange in his Voisin biplane.

Penaud, Alphonse French, built first elastic-driven propeller model airplane (1871).

Post, Wiley U.S. flyer who with Harold Gatty

U.S. pilot Wiley Post's long-distance feats are recorded on the side of the Winnie Mae.

flew around the world in 1931. In 1933 became the first solo pilot to circle the globe.

Quimby, Harriet U.S. flyer, first woman pilot to fly the English Channel (1912).

Rodgers, Calbraith Perry U.S. flyer, first pilot to cross the U.S. from east to west (1911).

Santos-Dumont, Albert Brazilian flyer who experimented with airships and in 1906 made the first airplane flight in Europe.

Scott, Sheila British flyer, the first European woman to fly solo around the world (1966). In 1971 she made the first solo flight in a light plane over the North Pole. She died in 1988.

Selfridge, William First person to die in an airplane crash (September 17, 1908).

Smith, Elinor American pilot who, at the age of 17, set an endurance record in 1929 by flying for almost 26 1/2 hours. At 15 she had her pilot's license suspended for flying beneath the East River bridges in Manhattan.

Smith, Keith and Ross Australian brothers, flew from Britain to Australia in 1919 (27 days, 20 hours overall, including stops).

Solar Challenger First human-powered airplane to fly the English Channel, piloted by Paul MacCready (1981).

von Hunefeld, Baron German leader of first flight east to west across the Atlantic (1928); 36 1/2 hours in the air from Ireland to the Straits of Belle Isle (Newfoundland/Labrador).

Warsitz, Erich German pilot of the world's first jet plane, the He 178 (August 27, 1939).

Whitehead, Gustav German pioneer, working in the U.S., who is said to have flown before the Wrights, in 1901.

Wright, Wilbur and Orville Constructed first airplane, *Flyer No. 1*, to achieve powered, human-carrying flight, covering a distance of 120 feet (1903).

Yeager, Charles U.S. pilot, first person to fly supersonically, in the Bell X-1 rocket plane (1947).

Zambeccarri, Count Italian balloonist who lost several fingers from frostbite when flying at high altitude, and died in 1812 when his combination balloon caught fire. He jumped from the basket at treetop height, but was killed by the fall.

IMPORTANT DATES IN AVIATION HISTORY

1783 First balloon ascent, by J.F. Pilâtre de Rozier and Marquis d'Arlandes in France.

1785 J-P. Blanchard flies the English Channel in a balloon.

1852 Henri Giffard builds a steam-powered airship.

1853 Cayley's coachman flies in his master's glider.

1884 Charles Renard and A.C. Krebs design an improved airship.

1891 Otto Lilienthal begins his gliding experiments.

1902 Wright brothers fly their No. 3 glider.

1903 Wrights' *Flyer* makes the first powered airplane flight.

1909 Louis Blériot flies the English Channel.

1919 Alcock and Brown fly the Atlantic nonstop.

1927 Lindbergh makes first solo flight from U.S. to Europe.

1929 *Graf Zeppelin* airship flies around the world.

1939 First jet plane; Germany's He 178.

1947 Bell X-1 is first plane to fly faster than sound.

1949 First nonstop round-the-world flight, by USAF B-50 (refueled in flight).

1969 First flight of the supersonic airliner Concorde.

1978 First balloon crossing of the Atlantic; by Ben Abruzzo, Maxie Anderson, and Larry Newman in *Double Eagle 2*.

1981 Space Shuttle *Columbia* launched.

1986 *Voyager* makes the first nonstop unrefueled flight around the world.

□ INDEX □